Table of Contents

I HUMBLY ASK YOU, IN
HUMILITY, TO
PLEASE ASK THE HOLY SPIRIT
FOR DISCERNMENT
BEFORE READING THIS BOOK.
MAY GOD BLESS YOU GREATLY.

Confirmation

of

Truth

HOW WOULD YOUR LIFE BE
IF YOU
FOUND A WAY
TO HAVE FAVOR WITH GOD
THAT
WORKED
GARY WILLIAMS

DEDICATION

I dedicate this book to Jesus Christ, my God, my Savior, my Lord, and my friend who answered my prayer to Him years ago for a closer relationship. I wanted to know Jesus better, I wanted to feel His presence, I wanted to hear Him clearly in prayer, and throughout my daily life. It is my desire, Lord, that through the obedience of writing this book, many would understand why you sent Kevin Zadai back to be the bridge that many would walk across in these last days. Your word, Lord, is always True, and you will leave the ninety-nine to save the one. I thank you, Lord, for loving me more than I could ever understand and for providing me, as well as many others, a way to grow so much in such a short time. You have opened my eyes to truth through seeking a relationship with you first, and above all things, favor can be had without the asking.

Matthew 6:33 The Passion Translation (TPT)

33 "So above all, constantly chase after the realm of God's kingdom, and the righteousness that proceeds from him. Then all these less important things will be given to you abundantly."

ACKNOWLEDGMENTS

I would like to thank Kevin Zadai for his obedience to Jesus in coming back, as well as being a bridge for so many people who needed him outside of just me, and Kyle McWhirter for assisting in the final editing of this book. I would also like to thank Kathi Zadai, Jesse & Kathi Duplantis and Sid Roth for their faithfulness to God in these last days as it is through their obedience Jesus will be able to reach so many. In partnering with Kevin God has created a mighty force to be reckoned with in this Kingdom age for the salvation of souls. All of you, as well as Kathi Zadai, who was chosen by God to be Kevin's wife and partner in faith for this special mission, are of vital importance in bringing the body of Christ into agreement with God. It is us, the body of Christ who are to put Jesus' enemies at His feet as a footstool, and it is my honor to have men and women such as you lead the way in these last days. I would also like to thank my wife Rita, given to me by the Lord, who has gifts in abundance that I lack, and without her my journey would have been much more difficult to make. She is my best friend outside of you Lord, and my confirmation in many things; you know me better than I know myself, and you knew that the gifts you had put in each of us would be of great use and strength to each other. You amaze me at every turn, and I will never be able to thank you enough for everything you have done for me throughout my life – as if my Salvation wasn't enough. Glory be to you God, forever and ever, Amen!

INTRODUCTION

Favor with God is something we can all have – we just need to know that God already wants to give us the desires of our heart. I mean, that's why we were created in the first place, right? So that God could have a family that He would love and provide for.

Think about it, what did Adam and Eve ever lack?

Genesis 1:26 New Living Translation (NLT)

26 Then God said, "Let us make human beings in our image, to be like us. They will reign over the fish in the sea, the birds in the sky, the livestock, all the wild animals on the earth, and the small animals that scurry along the ground."

Genesis 2:15-17 New Living Translation (NLT)

15 The Lord God placed the man in the Garden of Eden to tend and watch over it. 16 But the Lord God warned him, "You may freely eat the fruit of every tree in the garden— 17 except the tree of the knowledge of good and evil. If you eat its fruit, you are sure to die."

I was told by Jesus to write a book and share my walk with others, who like me, were searching for a closer relationship with Him. Jesus brought Kevin Zadai into my life almost 4 years ago to help me learn how to have favor with Him, and it was through Kevin that Jesus spoke His Truths to me. Twice I went to Him in prayer and asked, "Lord is Kevin who I should be listening to?" and twice I was told the same thing, "Kevin is of me, listen to him, and apply the Truths I reveal to you to your life." Since that day, I have done just that, and this book is a confirmation of what happened in my life after I did, and the journey God took me on to get there.

Chapter 1

In the Beginning

I remember almost five years ago, I started on a journey to become closer to God – even though I had known Jesus my whole life. As a child I was brought up in a Lutheran church, though I had never had a relationship with Jesus, I just knew that He was the Son of God and that I needed Him for my salvation.

Over the years I drifted further and further away from Him, coming back for only short periods of time here and there. I went through countless troubling times in my life over those years: the death of a woman whom I deeply loved, a divorce much later in my life that left me raising my daughter on my own, as well as many other trials.

Looking back over the years, I discovered that the majority of the time I went back to God throughout my journey, they were in periods of my life when I needed Him most...He was always there for me; I just wasn't always there for Him.

It was much later in life that I began to feel like I was missing something, that there was more to me and my life than what I had always perceived there to be. I began to search for more. To search for something, I knew was missing but wasn't quite sure what it was. I knew God was always there, I just didn't know how to have more of Him in my life.

I began to feel that I was more than what I thought I was. I felt like I had hidden abilities within me that would aid me in my relationship with God if I could only get them to manifest, which in turn led me to a deeper search within myself. I knew that deep inside there was something more, so I began to research information online that I thought could assist me in getting there.

I started out with different forms of meditation, listening to different types of music, modifying my diet with different foods and supplements, as well as drinking only deionized, filtered water. In my search for information, I began to discover that there were many things that were linked together in one way or another and as my search grew so did the topics, I found myself having an interest in.

I began to research history and fill my head with various types of information concerning alien life and ancient historic structures. I was on a quest for the truth. I wanted to find myself and tap into the true nature of what I was capable of. I knew deep inside me that I was so much more than the world had told me I was.

I would spend hours upon hours watching different historic documentaries on aliens and ancient structures such as Puma Punku, Machu Picchu, Stonehenge, the Pyramids of Giza, and others... I watched videos and read articles about people who claimed to work for top-secret government programs, the underground facilities that exist unknown to the public and different types of advanced technology these facilities have been working on over the years. Everything from cloning, time travel and telepathy, to mind-projection and out-of-body travel. A particle collider (CERN), or so they claim it is... A weather controller (HAARP), and the theories of different dimensions. These government facilities were in contact with supposed ancient alien life such as the Reptilians, the Nordics, the Greys, the Annunaki, the Adromedans, the Pleiadians, and more; stating they were underground and in the oceans throughout various hidden places in the world. It was amazing the complex network of information and how it was all woven together.

I began to research who the Illuminati and the Freemasons were. The rich elites of the world like the Rothschilds, Rockefellers,

CONFIRMATION OF TRUTH

Oppenheimers, Goldsmid/Goldschmidt, George Soros...how they and the Federal Reserve tie in with all of this. But REMEMBER I had an open mind, and I was just in search of the truth as I believed that if I knew the truth the end result would be the ability to operate at a higher level within myself, and to have a closer relationship with God. The more I discovered, the more I began to realize what a lie everything in the world really was.

I remember when I prayed to God I would always ask and hope to feel His presence. After leaving my house for work I would also say to myself "Today I'm going to have a perfect day for God, I will not get involved in any idol conversation that I should not be involved in. I will focus on being a good person." As you may have guessed, I would fail every day within the first hour of being there. I then put a picture of Jesus on my phone to remind me to be a better person as we all spend too much time each day looking at our phones, and as you may have guessed again, I would fail within the first hour of being there.

Over time I started to see that I just could not get to the place I wanted to be no matter how hard I tried. I would think to myself, "I have gained all this knowledge, and I have learned more truth than I had ever known before." So, what am I doing wrong except adding fear to my life? Yes, the more truth that I discovered the more I didn't like what I was learning. I began to fear the evil in the world as my eyes were being opened to more of what was really there. I started to stock up on food and water. I bought weapons. I would watch survival videos as my purpose now was to be prepared for what I knew was to come. Of course, my quest to be closer to God had not changed, but my knowledge of the world had. Based on these facts I had learned over time, I felt I had to be prepared, that God was showing me these truths so that I would be ready for what was to come, or was He?

Now, let's talk about my wife, who is a blessing given to me by God. She was raised in a Catholic church and believed in God, as well as Salvation through Jesus Christ just as I did. The one thing my wife and I both had in common at this stage in our lives was the search for more. My wife and I knew in our hearts that there was something we both were missing but just couldn't figure out what it was. She had questions concerning the Catholic church and what she had been taught growing up over the years. I had questions concerning a deeper truth that I felt was there but, was being hidden by the elites of the world. Yes, I believed that there was something more out there, and I was determined to find out what it was.

As my knowledge grew so did my fear of the world. I would of course always fall back on the notion that knowledge is power and that God had shown me these truths so that I would be ready for what was to come. But I also needed to share some of this knowledge with her so that if, and when things ever become really bad, she would be somewhat prepared. I did not share with her everything I had learned, because I did not want to scare her. I had learned of these things over time, and I knew her choking point was way too low.

My wife has always been a great supporter of me and my endeavors. She has an open mind like I do, and if it makes sense, it makes sense... This I believe would turn out to be one of the main reasons the Lord put us together in the first place, as we both have incredibly open minds; together we make a better person – where I am lacking in strength, she is not and where she is lacking in strength, I am not. We share a great respect for one another and value each other's opinions and I believe it is because of this type of relationship we are able to grow as individuals but mature together as one and it will prove to be of great value in each other's future as we both pursue a closer walk with the Lord.

My wife knew that I was on some type of quest for knowledge and that the purpose was to reach a higher state of being so that I could have a closer walk with God. In fact, many times she would join me in my endeavors just to see where it would lead. I would always share with her what I thought I was learning: the meditation, the different types of music, modification of diet with supplements and different foods designed to enhance one's state of being, the drinking of only deionized water. The only things I didn't share with her like I mentioned earlier were the negative things I was discovering along the way, the things that I thought might scare her, as she is a very positive person and did not like to be exposed to negative things. I figured I would bring her along slowly by introducing her to little bits over time.

Many things that I was discovering just didn't make sense. I mean, how were all these ancient structures across the world created during the time they were? Puma Punku, Stonehenge, Machu Picchu, The Pyramids of Giza... Structures that in some cases were made at a time when humans didn't even have the skills or tools to make such things. For example, the largest stone block in Puma Punku is 7.81 meters long, 5.17 meters wide, and is approximately 1.07 meters thick, the estimated weight is around 131 tons – the second largest block found within the complex weighs in at an estimated 85.21 tons and, the precision with which these blocks have been cut create joints so flush that not even a razor blade can fit between the stones. These structures were built with such precision that only a society with the knowledge of sophisticated stone-cutting skills and advanced mathematics could have built them. This is just a single example of the countless mysteries in the world, and if you research long enough you begin to discover that there is indeed a cover-up of the truth.

Knowledge is power, and there are many high-level people in the world who would like to use this knowledge for their own benefit, their own agenda. The real question is, what are they really hiding from the masses, and it is that question that leads me further into my research for the truth.

It was at this point in my life that I came to the realization that God was possibly leading me on a journey of discovery, a journey that would take many twists and turns as I continue to dive deeper and deeper into the mystery of who I am and what I am really capable of. I know in my heart that there is more, and something is being hidden. I just haven't found out what that something is yet.

We live in an age like no other, with access to knowledge that is readily available for anyone who is willing to take the time to look. I am that person because I want to know.

Chapter 2

An Unexpected Place

The meditation is not really taking me where I want to go, at least not the type of meditation I am doing. I begin to question everything, the motives behind the untruths and the secrets the world leaders are hiding from the general population. In meditation one often listens to music and chants at various frequencies to help achieve a higher state of being. Through my research I have discovered that there are positive and negative frequencies.

"If you want to find the secrets of the universe, think in terms of energy, frequency and vibration." Nikola Tesla

In my research I found there were experiments done that showed not only could you levitate objects through acoustics-resonance-frequency, but you could also destroy things as well. For example, how an opera singer can break a crystal glass with the high-pitched sound of their voice. I also discovered that through resonance by way of a tone generator it was possible to place salt on a flat, metal plate and through resonance, cause it to vibrate in such a way that it would create geometric patterns that would continue to increase in complexity as the pitch of the tone increased.

Over time I also discovered a researcher by the name of Dr. Masaru Emoto, who referenced the power of words, images, and frequencies, and their influence on water. Dr. Emoto, would expose water to various things like music, spoken words, typed words, pictures and videos; he would then crystallize it to see what the waters response would be, the response was amazing. Words like Happiness, Appreciation, Gratitude, Love, Peace, and Truth, as well as Holy Water, Positive Prayer and the presence of a young child produced beautiful crystals. Phrases like, 'I will kill you', 'you make me sick' and the words, demon, anger and Adolph Hitler would produce crystals that were polluted and deformed. When the water was exposed to music like "Amazing Grace," and Beethoven's *Pastoral* it produced beautiful crystals. When it was exposed to music like heavy metal, the crystals again would be polluted and deformed.

The mysteries and deeper truths are now coming to the surface as things I never expected to discover are being presented to me. In my search for a closer relationship with God I begin to ask myself, where is He taking me? In the Bible the book of Matthew (7:7-8) says,

Matthew 7: 7-8 (TPT)

7 *"Ask, and the gift is yours. Seek, and you'll discover. Knock, and the door will be opened for you. 8 For every persistent one will get what he asks for. Every persistent seeker will discover what he longs for. And everyone who knocks persistently will one day find an open door."*

I knew in my heart that if I would look for God with a passion, that He would not deny me the truth, and so my journey continued.

As I dove deeper and deeper into my research of meditation, I tended to gravitate more toward the Zen and Kundalini types, focusing on the seven chakras and the development of my pineal gland. I was convinced there was some type of ability being hidden from me due to a lack of use, caused by the fluorides in our water supply that would create calcification over time – another theory put out there... This was a belief that the governments or higher-ups were causing this intentionally to hide something that they did not want the masses to know.

As I mentioned earlier, I changed my diet to only purified deionized water and organic foods. I began including supplements like turmeric curcumin, liquid iodine, food grade hydrogen peroxide, fermented cod liver oil, food grade borax... I would meditate for long periods of time, listening to different chants and frequencies trying to reach a higher state of consciousness, which I believed at the time would help me to hear God more clearly. But as I continued my research, I began to discover the other side of things and started to distrust the frequencies I was listening to all together, after viewing a show on how Adolph Hitler used broadcast frequency 440hz to create anger and rage in people before he spoke. He also played a great part in the decision of the IOS (International Organization for Standardization) in setting the tuning standard to A440 due to his powerful influence.

With this information of the influence of frequency on the mind I began to ask myself, how do I know the music I'm listening to is really a safe frequency? How do I know it's even the frequency that it's stated to be? How do I know that the chants I listen to have no underlying message implanted in them? I began to distrust many things, the more I learned the more I discovered that many of the things I was researching held a darker side.

At this point, I did not give up mediation, but I was very careful as to what I would listen to, making sure that it came from a Christian source I felt was trustworthy. I mean, I was too scared to listen to anything else. I began to come across stories of people who were having negative encounters while experimenting with out-of-body experiences called, astral projection. Several of these people said they had some type of spirit guide, saw things or beings they couldn't explain, also stating these beings could see them as well and were aware of their presence. I found stories of the military's use of this type of meditation and that they had enhanced the experience with the use of technological equipment. Some of the stories were so far out there it would blow your mind to think that these things were even possible, but the credibility of the people who were telling the stories seemed reliable. They were either people who used to have high level jobs in the government, or friends and family members of people who did, and it was at this time I began to look deeper into what the military was doing with similar types of technology. The more I researched one area, the further it would lead me to somewhere else – just one rabbit hole after another and the curious thing was that it all seemed to be linked together.

As I began to dive deeper into these other topics alien life, the ancient historic structures, advanced technologies, giant people and even parallel dimension/time travel theories; I found myself blown away, I mean these things just seemed so amazing to me. There were so many opinions out there that it was becoming more and more difficult to determine what was true and what was not. I knew one thing though, that there were powerful people keeping secrets from the masses, and I was determined to find out what they were. I mean, if only a fraction of the stuff I was discovering was true, that would be enough to rock anyone's world.

I had always believed in alien life based on what I knew about the Bible. My view on alien life was as such that God had created many things besides man, and the understanding I had of this comes from reading two sections of scripture.

Throne of God in Revelations 7: 11-12.

Revelations 7: 11-12 (TPT)

11. All the angels were standing in a circle around the throne with the elders, and the four living creatures, and they all fell on their faces before the throne and worshiped God, 12. singing:

"Amen! Praise and glory,

wisdom and thanksgiving,

honor, power, and might

belong to our God forever and ever! Amen!"

Revelations 4: 4, 6-8.

Revelation 4: 4 6-8 (TPT)

John's Vision of the Throne Room

4 Encircling the great throne were twenty-four thrones with elders in glistening white garments seated upon them, each wearing a golden crown of victory.

Worship around the Throne

6 And in front of the throne there was pavement like a crystal sea of glass. Around the throne and on each sidestood four living creatures, full of eyes in front and behind. 7 The first living creature resembled a lion, the second an ox, the third had a human face, and the fourth was like an eagle in flight. 8 Each of the four living creatures had six wings, full of eyes all around and under their wings. They worshiped without ceasing, day and night, singing,

"Holy, holy, holy is the Lord God, the Almighty!

The Was,the Is,and the Coming!"

Here were examples to me of other beings that God had created. Given this information, and considering the vastness of creation, I came to the conclusion that God must have created other beings throughout the universe, but the one unique thing about human beings was that we were the only thing ever created out of His likeness. We are special and knowing this always gave me a sense of comfort and honor to be so uniquely special to God. It would not be until later in my life that I would discover I was close in my understanding but not quite correct in my overall view of what was really true. At that stage in my life, I just didn't know how profound the reality of it really was; I was not only special, but I was a child of the living God.

My research on alien life took me in many different directions, from the Roswell, New Mexico incident and the conspiracy of a crashed UFO and aliens recovered by our government, to discoveries of an alleged crashed ship and a female body found on the moon – not to mention the claims of abandoned buildings found as well. There were so many stories of things being discovered that have been hidden from the public that it would easily overwhelm you. There are stories like the US Navy, Antarctica expedition in 1946/47, where a fleet comprised of around 4,700 military personnel, an aircraft carrier (the USS Philippine Sea, one of the largest carriers at the time), and many naval support ships and aircraft got into a battle with a group of UFOs that ended with great loss and many deaths. The man leading the expedition Admiral Richard Byrd, was quickly silenced after telling his story of the events that took place – an article written later in *New Dawn* by Frank Joseph also gave a very detailed analysis of two eyewitness accounts stating what had happened as well as what they saw. As many of the stories I was coming a crossed began to build so did the information I was discovering the deep, underground bases throughout the United States, and experiments taking place around the globe in nearly every scientific field imaginable, antigravity, time travel, astral projection, genetic alterations and enhancements, advanced cloning, weather control (HAARP), access to dimensional portals with an advanced tech called CERN. There are stories of certain bodies of our government working with groups around the world, having affiliations and alliances with these so-called alien beings and unknown entities in an exchange for more advanced technologies than humankind is currently capable of.

Below is a list of the most well-known alien races which are in fact to my knowledge demons, and principalities in high places:

Zeta Reticulans or "Grey Aliens"

- Little green men
- Nordic aliens
- Pleiadian aliens
- Andromedan aliens
- Reptilian aliens
- Alpha Draconian
- Sirian aliens
- Anunnaki aliens
- Arcturian aliens

CONFIRMATION OF TRUTH

There are even stories of unique and giant beings, as well as ancient ruins found at different locations throughout the world. Structures that defy logic, some dating back as far as 16,000 years, so they say.

Unique and Giant Beings

- Giant skeleton of Bulgaria estimated to be around 6,500 years old
- The 3,000-year-old Paracas skulls
- Ancient giant bones of Sardinia
- Homo naledi found in a cave complex in South Africa
- The Atacama alien skeleton

Ancient Ruins

- Mayan city of Chichén Itzá
- Stonehenge of Wiltshire, England
- Puma Punku in Tiahuanaco, Bolivia
- The Great Pyramid of Giza
- Romanian Rock Cut Cave, Megalithic ruins

These are just a few examples of a wealth of information that can be found in books and on the internet concerning these stories and countless more. If you look to the book of Numbers: 13, in the time of Moses, one can see a glimpse of what was on the Earth in those days.

Numbers 13 1-2 33 (NLT)

Twelve Scouts Explore Canaan

1 The LORD now said to Moses,2 "Send out men to explore the land of Canaan, the land I am giving to the Israelites. Send one leader from each of the twelve ancestral tribes."

The Scouting, Report?

33 We even saw giants there, the descendants of Anak. Next to them we felt like grasshoppers, and that's what they thought, too!"

Genesis 6: 4

4 Very large men were on the earth in those days, and later also, when the sons of God lived with the daughters of men, who gave birth to their children. These were the powerful men of long ago, men of much strength. According to the Book of Numbers, **Anak** was a forefather of the Anakim. The **Bible** describes them as very tall descendants of Anak. The text states that the Anakim were Rephaites, and that **Anak** was a son of Arba.

Arba was a man who is mentioned in the Book of Joshua. In Joshua 14:15, he is called the *"greatest man among the Anakites."* Joshua 15:13 says, *Arba was the father of Anak.* The Anakites are described in the Hebrew Bible as giants.

The sons of God are from the line of Seth and were influenced by the Nephilim to interbreed with the daughters of men. The Nephilim are "Fallen Angels who are now chained by God awaiting judgement." See Jude 6

I found that there is a lot of controversy on this but no angel has ever been a Son of God. Jesus is the Son of God and we are God's children it's that simple. Read Hebrews 1 and 2 if you have questions.

I found amazing information concerning technologies, such as HAARP and CERN.

HAARP like I've mentioned earlier being a weather control device in Gakona, Alaska, rumored to have the ability to not only control the weather but cause earthquakes as well. CERN was very concerning, as it is a massive Hadron collider which collides protons or subatomic particles into each other at nearly the speed of light and is said to have possibly created a new particle called the 'ghost particle'. The machine was made originally to look for what is called the 'God particle' (Higgs Boson), as well as study the origins of the universe. There are rumors that some scientists claim they have been able to open a doorway and tap into other dimensions. The true purpose behind CERN is not what they are telling the public, which makes it all the more dangerous.

CONFIRMATION OF TRUTH

Then I came to the Vatican. All their secrets and all the ancient artifacts they have been said to have confiscated over the years – not to mention the Large Telescope they named, lucifer. The Illuminati, the Freemasons (which in reality are rumored to be the elites of the world), the Rockefellers, the Rothschilds, the Du Pont Family, the Astors, the Freemans, the Russells, etc... They are the families with all the money; the families who own a group of banks and have heavy ties to the Federal Reserve. These families have also been rumored and linked to nearly everything regarding what I spoke about earlier. Money and knowledge is power. It's that simple.

Which begs the next question...Are all the things I've discovered on my journey true? Maybe, maybe not. But again the credibility of the sources are good, and in some cases almost too good. As I have mentioned earlier, we live in an era where information is readily available to anyone who is willing to take the time to look.

Unfortunately, my journey of discovery ended up leading me to dark places I didn't like, and I was no closer to God than I was when I started.

Chapter 3

A Place of Fear

As I continue with my meditation techniques under the illusion that it was bringing me into a closer relationship with God, I also became aware of the paranoia I was beginning to feel from everything I had learned in my search for the truth. I started to worry about the evil in the world and what I believe its ultimate plan is; the plan for power and control under a one world government. I start to recognize through more research that there is a corruption in our government called, the 'Deep State', who are in the back pockets of the elites of the world. They are the ones tied to satanism, the Illuminati, the Freemasons, the Vatican, and the advanced technologies and underground networks throughout the world; those with all the money...

It was around this time Donald Trump announced his run for Presidency that I started to realize what was truly going on. I began to discover things about the Deep State and their ties to the elite that were truly evil. An evil so dark that I will not include it in this book as it would serve no purpose other than putting terrible images and thoughts into your mind. What I will say and said earlier is that out of fear I started to do things to protect myself and my family, like stocking up on food and supplies as well as other things. I knew something terrible was coming, and I was not entirely sure how to handle it

2 Timothy 1:7 (TPT)

⁷For God will never give you the spirit of fear, but the Holy Spirit who gives you mighty power, love, and self-control.

I prayed to God that President Trump would be elected as I somehow knew in my heart that he was the right person. He was not a politician, he had a pedigree background, and was a very successful businessman. This in my opinion made him the best choice for the job as he was not in the back pocket of the elites and was already a self-made billionaire. In reality, he really had nothing to gain by running other than his love for the United States. I began to see lies, deception, and manipulation in our government like never before. I saw that some of our elected leaders had no loyalty to America or its people as they were only concerned with doing what the elites had paid them to do. The elites own them; it is that simple. It even goes as far as family connections; some of these elite individuals have family members who are public officials residing in positions of power in our government.

It was a complete mystery to me as to how some of the people around me I considered to be insightful, logical and held common sense, could not see what I was seeing plain as day. Evil and perversion was starting to run rampant in our society as the rule of law was being taken down by the very system that had put it in place. Perversion began to enter all of our favorite Hollywood shows and movies, and without question became socially acceptable by the masses; lawlessness was everywhere as mentally unstable people and violent groups like Antifa, and BLM began to spring up, God's word clearly says we are to obey the laws and have respect for governmental authority see **Romans 13** and that he does not show favoritism as all lives matter to Him see **Romans 2: 11**. Corruption was even starting to show throughout our judicial system and the media, as lies were being sold for the truth, and truth replaced with lies.

A narrative was being let loose on our society, and it wasn't good. It became evident that our society as a whole was beginning to turn away from God – such as the removal of the Ten Commandments from outside courthouses and government properties. New genders were popping up all over and homosexuality was being sold as the new norm. Homelessness was becoming a rampant problem in many states, and a country that had been founded on the principles of God, was now watching its moral fabric being torn in half. I remember asking myself why there were so many people who did not see this? Then I remembered a verse of scripture from the New Testament, in the book of Romans.

Romans 1: 28 (TPT)

28 And because they thought it was worthless to embrace the true knowledge of God, God gave them over to a worthless mind-set, to break all rules of proper conduct.

Yes, a new narrative was being formed in this country right before my very eyes, and its purpose was to destroy what had been created by our Founding Fathers. It was converting the United States into a third world country, stripping it of all its morality, self-sufficiency, and ability to defend itself. How do you take down the most powerful country in the world? Not with might, but by destroying it from within itself, taking down the very framework that makes it strong, then by turning the people against themselves, and stripping the society of its history and all morality.

The new secret weapon of evil was in the phrase **"politically correct."** Conforming to a belief that language and practices which could offend political sensibilities (as in matters of sex or race) should be eliminated. This was a well-thought-out plan by some very evil people, put in process many years ago, and now coming to full maturity. In the wake of all these terrible things that I had discovered in my search for truth, there was one thing I had not forgotten. I had not forgotten the reason I had started this journey in the first place, to discover more about myself and the inner belief that there was more to me than I had been led to believe. There was truth that the world had blinded me to, but in my heart, I knew was there.

Though I had learned a lot more than I bargained for, and my life was now plagued with the unknown. I still had God, and I trusted that He would always be there to guide me as long as I truly had a desire in my heart to be close to Him.

Knowing what was really going on around me, I began to pray more often. I would pray to God (no, I would plead with God), to please let President Trump win this election to become the next president of the United States as I feared what would happen next if he lost. My support of Trump caused several of my friends to fall away and even created some turmoil with a few of my family members. I was still amazed at the fact that they could not see the evil going on around them. I mean, they believed in God and Jesus Christ as their savior, but had no relationship with Him, and to tell you the truth, my relationship with Him at that time was not the strongest either. For me personally, I believe the difference was that I was on a mission to know more, to know the truth, and to be closer to God. I truly believe that it was for this reason the Holy Spirit opened my eyes, so that I could see more clearly.

I can remember the day...I was sitting on my couch in front of my big-screen TV as the votes were coming in for the next president of the United States. It was one of the most hectic times of my life, and I'll never forget it. I knew there would be massive voter fraud involved and I felt a majority of it would most likely be tied to George Soros and the Democratic Party. But against all odds, and in a miracle of God's grace, Trump began to pull ahead of Clinton. It wasn't long after that my heart began to fill with joy as Trump had now become the next President of the United States. I knew at that very moment that even though this country and many of its churches had turned away from God, God had not turned away from us and that this was to be the beginning of a new Era for America. God was giving us a second chance to get it right.

It was about a year into Trump's Presidency that I realized the swamp was a lot bigger than I had initially thought. It wasn't just a swamp, it was an ocean of evil, and it was being seen in almost every branch of government we had. It was becoming blatantly apparent that there were people in our government who were owned by the elite on both sides of the fence, primarily in the Democratic party. However, both sides had Deep State players, and it was those same elite that owned 90 percent of our news networks such as CNN, MSN, MSNBC, CBS, etc... Outside of a small percentage of Fox News, I generally received most of my news on the internet from underground sources, and it was there that I discovered Q and the White Hats. They were said to be the good Christian people in our government that were in high places who talked Trump into running for President in the first place. They were on the front lines watching the infestation of evil throughout our government and are rumored to have come very close to taking down President Obama. They soon realized that without the support of the American people, their chances of success would be very small.

This was where the next phase of my journey began as I was now seeing just how much control the elites had established and stolen over the years, and not just in America, but throughout the world.

Again, I'll repeat myself was everything I was discovering true? Honestly, I don't know I guess that's something only the future can reveal, but I know what God was showing me in my spirit and the things being revealed were as real to me as the air I breath.

Chapter 4

Discernment Comes in Prayer

Filled with the relief that God had just answered mine and millions of other people's prayers with the election of Donald J. Trump as President of the United States, my journey was about to take a new turn, just as our new President was about to face the unseen evil he was put in place for and elected to defeat.

Thanking God in prayer for saving us from the disasters that would have certainly befallen America had Hillary Clinton won, I spent the rest of my day searching YouTube for information that would further my journey in a closer walk with God. It was at this moment in my life I began to see a pattern and started to reflect on the journey I had taken up to this point and reviewed all the places it had led me and all the knowledge I had uncovered in that process. I thought to myself, "is God trying to show me something He wants me to, see? Could there be more to all of this than what I actually thought?"

Based on where I was spiritually at this point in my life, I felt compelled for some odd reason to search out stories of life after death experiences, starting my search on YouTube. I just wanted to hear what people had to say. I was curious, I guess. I began to search, watching story after story, and was amazed by what I was hearing, many of these stories were very moving, and the emotion coming from these people was so intense it was as if they were re-living the experience all over again as they were sharing it.

I began to watch as many life after death experiences as I could find, comparing all the stories with one another, as well as searching scripture to see if these people were saying things that were out of context. My focus was now starting to turn more toward the Bible, where it should have been all along. I would take the videos that I was finding and focus on what they all had in common, as I believed the truth would lie in the commonality of the stories as long as it wasn't in conflict with scripture.

Not long after I had started my search for these types of stories did, I come across a man I had never heard of before by the name of Sid Roth. He was the host of the show, '***Sid Roth's It's Supernatural!***' on the ISN network. There was a guest on his show by the name of Kevin Zadai, who in 1992 had died during a routine surgery and met Jesus in the operating room. Jesus not only spoke to him, but took him to the other side as well, showing and teaching him many things. I was amazed by not just what I was hearing but what I was feeling inside of me as I was hearing it. It was something that I had never felt before in my life. I watched his story over and over, listening to every detail, and by this point my focus had now transferred to him.

I began to search for stories under the name Kevin Zadai, listening to every word he said in hopes of hearing something new, my mind was like a sponge, glued to his every word. Story after story I would listen, finally coming to the realization that this was where God had been leading me all along. Kevin was the real deal, a gift of Jesus to the world as Jesus was speaking through him. I remember Jesus telling him, "Kevin if you go back for me, you can't lose, I will be at your right side every time you speak, and I will tell you what to say."

When I think about the New Testament, the authority and wisdom with which Jesus spoke, and how it affected the people as well as the religious leaders and scholars of the day, it brings me to sections of scripture in **Mark 1: 21-28** and **Luke 4: 16-22**

Mark 1: 21-28 (NLT)

Jesus Casts Out an Evil Spirit

21Jesus and his companions went to the town of Capernaum. When the Sabbath day came, he went into the synagogue and began to teach. 22The people were amazed at his teaching, for he taught with real authority—quite unlike the teachers of religious law.

23 Suddenly, a man in the synagogue who was possessed by an evil spirit cried out, 24"Why are you interfering with us, Jesus of Nazareth? Have you come to destroy us? I know who you are—the Holy One of God!"

25 But Jesus reprimanded him. "Be quiet! Come out of the man," he ordered. 26 At that, the evil spirit screamed, threw the man into a convulsion, and then came out of him.

27Amazement gripped the audience, and they began to discuss what had happened. "What sort of new teaching is this?" they asked excitedly. "It has such authority! Even evil spirits obey his orders!" 28The news about Jesus spread quickly throughout the entire region of Galilee.

Luke 4: 16-22 (NLT)

16 When he came to the village of Nazareth, his boyhood home, he went as usual to the synagogue on the Sabbath and stood up to read the Scriptures. 17The scroll of Isaiah the prophet was handed to him. He unrolled the scroll and found the place where this was written:

18 "The Spirit of the Lord is upon me,

for he has anointed me to bring Good News to the poor.

He has sent me to proclaim that captives will be released,

that the blind will see,

that the oppressed will be set free,

19 and that the time of the Lord's favor has come."

20He rolled up the scroll, handed it back to the attendant, and sat down. All eyes in the synagogue looked at him intently. 21 Then he began to speak to them. "The Scripture you've just heard has been fulfilled this very day!"

22Everyone spoke well of him and was amazed by the gracious words that came from his lips. "How can this be?" they asked. "Isn't this Joseph's son?" This in my opinion is why I and so many others were so drawn to Kevin. When listening to him speak, it was like listening to the authority and wisdom of Jesus Himself because that's what it is; Jesus speaking His words of truth through him. The words of life.

In all my life I have never heard anyone speak with such knowledge and truth in the body of Christ. Jesus is in him because it is as Kevin says, "I'm not that good."

It wasn't long after that I introduced my wife Rita to Kevin, and at first, she was a little hesitant, but I remembered the deal that Kevin had made with Jesus before he agreed to come back. Kevin, told Jesus that if he agreed to do this for Him it had to stick. When people left after hearing what Kevin had to say for the Lord, they would not fall away, but be transformed inside forever.

With this fore knowledge, I knew that it would not take long to get my wife on board. We were both looking for answers to the same questions at this stage in our lives, and Kevin's deal with Jesus was true. My wife's life was soon transformed just as mine had and continued to do so. We began to watch Kevin together almost every day and applied all the things we were learning to our lives. We had both been changed forever just as Jesus had told Kevin it would be.

After listening to Kevin speak on many occasions over a period of about a year, I began to wonder, "Is this the path that God has chosen for me, is this the way I am to go?" Then I went into deep prayer, asking Jesus on two separate occasions, "Lord," I said, "are Kevin and his experiences really real? Lord, I am coming to you with an open heart, asking you for truth before I go all in. Is Kevin real, and are the stories that he tells true?" Jesus responded back to me both times with the exact same answer. "Kevin is from me, listen to him, and support him in everything that he does." I never asked Jesus that question again, and I did exactly what He asked me to do.

Later that week I set up a Facebook page, YouTube channel, and Twitter account all for the purpose of supporting Kevin Zadai and God's agenda. Not long after that he started the Warrior Notes School, at which my wife, and I were in the first group of 500 students to join. It was in this new direction my journey had taken me that everything was now beginning to fall into place.

For the first time in my life, I began to gain an understanding of who I really was in Jesus Christ. He was my truth, my salvation, my everything, and He was about to open my world to truths that were better than anything I could have ever imagined. For it is written:

1 Corinthians 2:9 (TPT)

9 This is why the Scriptures say: Things never discovered or heard of before, things beyond our ability to imagine—these are the many things God has in store for all his lovers.

Through the Holy Spirit who was living in me would come discernment. It was for many years I had felt that I was missing something, the truth of who I really was. I had this feeling deep inside that there were more hidden abilities within me that seemed to be spiritual in nature, and at the time I could not explain why as it was just a feeling that I had, but it was a strong feeling. Yes, strong enough to change the course of my life and start me on this journey in the first place.

Through this journey would come discovery, the discovery of many truths in the world being kept from the masses, secrets that those in power knew, but wanted to keep for themselves. It was in my desire to know more that I would come across these truths, and it was through this process of discovery that would eventually lead me back to Jesus Christ who had been waiting for me all along. The truth I had been searching for was in Him. Not some Zen or Kundalini meditation technique, or astral projection, or out of body experience.

It was Jesus who was my truth, my savior, my creator, my God, and in Him was the answer I had been searching for – the missing something that was more glorious than anything I could have imagined. You see, what I was to discover through the discernment of the Holy Spirit was that I was a spirit being created out of the likeness of God, with a soul, and housed in an organic body so that I could live in this world. I was a child of the living, Most High God, Creator of all things, and among those things created, I was special, the most valuable thing in Heaven as God loved me so much that He purchased me with His own blood.

John 3:16 The Passion Translation (TPT)

16 For this is how much God loved the world—he gave his one and only, unique Son as a gift.So now everyone who believes in him will never perish but experience everlasting life.

Genesis 1:26 (NLT)

26 Then God said, "Let us make human beings in our image, to be like us. They will reign over the fish in the sea, the birds in the sky, the livestock, all the wild animals on the earth, and the small animals that scurry along the ground."

Jeremiah 1:5 (NLT)

5 "I knew you before I formed you in your mother's womb. Before you were born, I set you apart and appointed you as my prophet to the nations."

John 17: 20-26 (TPT)

Jesus Prays for You

20 "And I ask not only for these disciples,
but also, for all those who will one day
believe in me through their message.
21 I pray for them all to be joined together as one
even as you and I, Father, are joined together as one.
I pray for them to become one with us
so that the world will recognize that you sent me.
22 For the very glory you have given to me I have given them
so that they will be joined together as one
and experience the same unity that we enjoy.
23 You live fully in me and now I live fully in them

so that they will experience perfect unity,
and the world will be convinced that you have sent me,
for they will see that you love each one of them
with the same passionate love that you have for me.
24 "Father, I ask that you allow everyone that you have given to me
to be with me where I am!
Then they will see my full glory—
the very splendor you have placed upon me
because you have loved me even before the beginning of time.
25 You are my righteous Father,
but the unbelieving world has never known you
in the perfect way that I know you!
And all those who believe in me
also know that you have sent me!
26 I have revealed to them who you are
and I will continue to make you even more real to them,
so that they may experience the same endless love
that you have for me, for your love will now live in them, even as I live in
them!

Chapter 5

A Relationship with God

Now that my eyes have been opened, my relationship with God begins to grow. It is at this point in my life I begin to feel like I have found a pot of gold; excitement and wonder begins to well up inside me as I continue reading scripture and learning of the deeper truths that Jesus is sharing with me through His words in scripture and Kevin Zadai. I begin to realize that through the applications of the teachings of Jesus and the submission of my will, not only am I building my eternal relationship with God, but my access to His almighty power and favor is endless.

I learn that my relationship with God is more important than anything else in my life, for it is through this relationship favor comes. I now understand that it is the basis for the very reason that God created me in the first place. God wanted a family to love and provide for, that freely worshiped and loved Him in return. It wasn't long after this that I made the commitment to Jesus that I would apply all the things I learned from Him through Kevin Zadai to my life. I wanted what Kevin had, one of the most favored lives and closest relationship with God that I had ever seen. The rest of this book will be a testament as to where that commitment to Jesus took me.

Matthew 6:33 (TPT)

33 So above all, constantly chase after the realm of God's kingdom and the righteousness that proceeds from him. Then all these less important things will be given to you abundantly.

Leviticus 26:12 (NLT)

12 I will walk among you; I will be your God, and you will be my people.

Psalm 8 (TPT)

5 Yet what honor you have given to men,

created only a little lower than Elohim,

crowned like kings and queens with glory and magnificence.

6 You have delegated to them

mastery over all you have made,

making everything subservient to their authority,

placing earth itself under the feet of your image-bearers.

7-8 All the created order and every living thing

of the earth, sky, and sea—

the wildest beasts and all the sea creatures—

everything is in submission to Adam's sons.

Filled with this knowledge and understanding, I now realized that if I just focus my attention on the realm of God's kingdom and the righteousness that proceeds from Him, I will have access to whatever I need without the asking as it will come to me through faith and relationship. I mean, God already knows what I need, right? I begin to feel as though I had discovered some secret biblical understanding, but it wasn't that at all. It was in plain sight right there in Matthew 6: 33. I just needed to understand the deeper meaning.

Thus far here is what I have learned to be true. I am a Spirit being, with a soul, and put into an organic body so that I can live in this realm. I am a child of the Living Most High God, created out of His likeness but living in a fallen state. My access to all He wants to give me lies in my relationship with Him through my Lord Jesus Christ, and if I seek Him first, placing God above all other things in my life, I can actually bring the Heavenly realm into this realm, subduing all things around me by learning to walk in the authority that Jesus bought for me through His resurrection. Yes, it could really be that easy and difficult at the same time.

I began to recall some of the things that Jesus had said to Kevin in their meeting after he had passed away during his operation, telling him that "people's prayers are strong, and that one of the most powerful things a person can do is to pray in the spirit or in tongues." He then used Kevin as an example by showing him just how effective he was as he prayed in the spirit. Jesus also told Kevin that one of the first things a person should focus on is finding out where they end, and he begins. You see, there is power available to all of us, but it's going to be by you losing and Him gaining. I began to understand what was meant when Jesus said in Matthew 16,

Matthew 16: 24-25 (TPT)

24 Then Jesus said to his disciples, "If you truly want to follow me, you should at once completely reject and disown your own life. And you must be willing to share my cross and experience it as your own, as you continually surrender to my ways." 25 For if you choose self-sacrifice and lose your lives for my glory, you will continually discover true life. But if you choose to keep your lives for yourselves, you will forfeit what you try to keep.

Pick up your cross and follow me. You see, one of the most important things I've learned thus far is that the submission of our will to God is one of the most important steps in gaining favor as well as bringing the Heavenly realm into this realm.

I knew that the submission of my will was going to be difficult, but I also knew that I did not have to attempt this on my own as I had the Father, Jesus, the Holy Spirit, and my Angels all at my disposal. I was not alone. I also knew that I had an additional secret weapon—praying in the spirit or in tongues—perfect prayer that would fill the gap of what I did not know to pray for. It would be praying in tongues that would help me in getting to that place where my books would be opened, and my destiny would start to unfold.

I began to pray more for other people, in fact I seldom prayed for myself except for God to help me in building my relationship with Him. I would pray for a relationship and tell The Father & Jesus how much I needed them. I would tell Jesus that I was well aware that apart from Him I could do nothing, but in Him I could do all things. I would set personal time aside during my week to ask God for nothing but his presence.

All I wanted was a personal relationship with God because I knew, for one, that was what I was created for in the first place, and two, I knew that through a personal relationship I could achieve all things without the asking, as God already knew what I needed and already wanted to give it to me anyway. Adam and Eve had a personal relationship with God, and what did they ever lack? Nothing! It was lucifer the liar convincing them that they had a lack that destroyed their relationship and caused them to fall from grace.

When I would come to a difficult point in my life, rather than asking God to solve it my way, I would just say, "Father, you know what I need, in Jesus' name amen." I trusted in my heart that God knew better than I did how to solve any problem that I may have. I gave Him the whole thing and trusted by faith. I found that this approach from Matthew 6: 33 would work better for me, as it would require me to trust even deeper in God's ability to know my needs and provide solutions. In fact, I would come to discover in the near future that I had many needs that were answered I had never asked for in the first place, they just happened. But I will save those miracles for a different section in this book, as they were the benefits that came from relationship.

I recall that as I learned to hear God speak to me in prayer over the years, I would sometimes question myself, "Did I really hear that right, and did God really tell me this?" It would be at times like this that God would do something miraculous, like I would watch a religious

TV program the same day or the following day, and it would be on the topic of what God was talking to me about earlier, and the answers would always be the same. I mean, exactly the same as if God was telling me the same thing again except this time through someone else. Well, I will tell you that after this happens to you over and over again, you stop questioning God and just learn to listen.

I will tell you this, how well I hear God always depended on me, my state of mind, and spirit, not Him. We all want to hear God audibly as it makes it easy, but whenever I would tell Jesus that I just wish I could hear Him clearly all the time, He would just respond back to me and say, "You hear me just fine." God speaks from our hearts where our spirit is, and for me He is a much quieter voice than mine, which is why it's so easy to talk over Him. Learning to quiet your mind and take every thought into captivity definitely helped me to hear God better.

I once received a message from Jesus for my daughter Ashley, and after the Lord had given me the message to give to her, which I wrote down on a notepad, He then told me that she would question as to how I heard Him, and the answer He told me to give her to this question was, "I am a voice that's a whisper with purpose and direction."

Yes, there are great benefits to having a relationship with God, and the more I learned from Jesus through Kevin Zadai and the scriptures, the more I would apply it to my life. You see, when you apply things and they start to work, your faith grows even stronger and you suddenly find yourself wanting more and more of God. He was my true Father, the one who actually created me, loved me beyond my ability to understand, so much that He would send His only begotten son to die for me so that I could come home, to my true home, and back into a perfect relationship with Him.

I wanted to know Him intimately and deeply. I wanted to someday walk into the eyes of Jesus as Kevin did and see that very moment in creation when I was thought into existence. I also knew that if I came to know God on a more intimate level, it would change me inside just like how being in the presence of God began to change Moses.

You see, I have become fully aware that I cannot change myself, but through the submission of my will and a relationship with God, I can trust that He will change me. It will be God Himself who will help me to become the spiritual being I was created to be in the first place, the true me, and not the me the world has always told me I am.

It is the moments in prayer late at night or on my days off early in the morning that I get to spend that special time with God. My days off are even more special as I pray very early in the morning before I do any of the things that I like to do, like having my coffee, listening to Christian music, and watching the birds on my back deck. I give God the first part of my day before I do anything. I wake up and say, "God your will be done today!" Then I say "Father I ask for and receive grace for today." This is how I pray.

I have a replica of the Ark of the Covenant with two candles on both sides. I light my candles, turn on my music by the Rivera's, then I bow my head, and ask the Holy Spirit to help me to pray to the Father with a pure and contrite heart, from there I ask the Father and Jesus my Lord to come and be with me, so I can feel their presence and their love. I tell them that I want to be with my family, to know them on a more intimate level.

I then say, "Father I know that you always hear me and that you're going to give me what I ask" I follow up with the Lord's prayer, then I pray for the safety of and for God's will to be done through President Trump and his White Hats as well as the Supreme Court and our Judiciary System. I also pray for his enemies, that they come to the loving knowledge and saving grace of Jesus Christ or be taken down and out of power. I do this because Jesus said to always pray for the President as well as the ones who are blinded by evil. I then move to my couch where I sit and say,

John 1 (NIV)

CONFIRMATION OF TRUTH

1 In the beginning was the Word, and the Word was with God, and the Word was God. 2 He was with God in the beginning. 3 Through him all things were made; without him nothing was made that has been made. 4 In him was life, and that life was the light of all mankind. 5 The light shines in the darkness, and the darkness has not overcome it.

Psalms 91 and **Psalms 51:12**

I live in the shelter of the Most High
I am under his shadow.
This I declare about the Lord:
He alone is my refuge, my place of safety.
He is my God, and I trust Him.
For He will rescue me from every trap, and protect me from deadly disease.
His faithful promises are my armor, and protection.
I will not be afraid of the terrors of the night, nor the arrow that flies in the day.
I will not dread the disease that stalks in darkness, nor the disaster that strikes at mid-day.
Though a thousand fall at my side, though ten thousand are dying around me, these evils
will not touch me.
When I open my eyes, I see how the wicked are punished.
Because I make the Lord my refuge, because I make the Most High my shelter,
No evil will conquer me; no plague will come near my home.
For He will order His angels to protect me wherever I go.
They will hold me up with their hands so I won't even hurt a foot on a stone.
I will trample upon lions and cobras; I will crush fierce lions, and serpents under my feet!
The Lord says,
"I will rescue those who love me.
I will protect those who trust in my name.

When they call on me, I will answer.
I will be with them in trouble.
I will rescue, and honor them.
I will reward them with a long life, and give them my salvation."
Then I read out loud this prayer:

"Father God, Psalm 148:13 says, let them praise the name of the Lord for his name alone is exalted. His Glory is above the Earth and Heaven. I praise you today. Your name alone is exalted high above every other name, King Jesus. I come before you today Father, seeking your presence to be with me, to go with me, to move with me. I seek your presence Lord because just as Moses asked "How then will it be known that I have found Grace in your sight, except if you go with us". Go with us today Lord I pray that your presence may go with us, surround us, and cover us. We need your presence Lord Jesus because in it we find Grace. In your Holy presence we find favor. We are made unique among other people. I pray for your presence to be with me, because in Psalm 16:11 your word says that you will show me the path of life. In your presence is fullness of joy. Joy that cannot be stolen from the enemy. Father I am chasing your presence today because it can protect me. It can keep me hidden from the attacks of the devil. The bible says in Psalm 31:20 you shall hide them in the secret place of your presence from the plots of man, you shall keep them securely from the strife of tongues. Hide me in your secret place, King Jesus. May I dwell there today and forever more. Father God my prayer is Psalm 51:10-12 where the bible says "create with in me a clean heart oh Father God and renew a steadfast spirit within me". Do not cast me away from your presence and do not take your Holy Spirit from me. Restore to me the joy of your salvations and uphold me by your generous spirit. I pray that you cleanse me from all sin Lord. Forgive me, so that there is nothing that will separate me from you in my life. I pray that the Holy Spirit leads me into the presence of God. May He install the right attitude within me. May He press on my heart the importance of God, so that I may be persistent in my prayers, persistent in asking God for his presence to go with me. I understand Lord that your

presence is not cheap. I need to be in the right standing with you. I need to be prayerful and persistent to push myself to seek and search for you always. Holy Spirit help me to consistently wait on the Lord. To constantly call on the name of Jesus. Hear my prayer Lord God Almighty and reveal yourself in my life. Reveal your Glory to me and my family. May your presence be with me each and every morning before I start my day and may it cover me and surround me even as I end my day. Be praised! Be honored! May you be worshiped and adored in my life, King Jesus. I thank you for listening to this prayer."

I then ask the Holy Spirit to pray for me in perfect prayer, and I begin to speak in tongues, as well as periodically going from tongues to exulting the Father for who He is, and how majestic, holy, and powerful He is, full of love, mercy, and grace. I will also thank Him for sending Jesus to save me and bring me home. I then begin to exalt Jesus for who and how awesome He is, and then I go back to praying in tongues. This can go on for an hour, sometimes two, and about three quarters of the way through, it happens. I feel the presence of God come over me, His peace, His love. It's like a warm loving energy all around me in a sea of peace. Sometimes things will be spoken to me, but most of the time it's just an unbelievable presence.

Now, I am not saying this is what you should do. I am only saying this is what I do, amongst many other things. I share this with you because it is at these times, I feel very close to God. Obviously, there is a lot more to prayer than just the prayer itself. There are also the facts of how you live your life: are you living for God or are you living for yourself? Do you tithe your income or your time? Do you read the word every day or often? Do you share the word, and are you kind to others, giving a hand to or helping the homeless? Do you go to church or belong to a Bible study group? These are just a list of some things you should think about if you do not already do them. This is what a relationship is: Jesus living through you, and we are all on our own walk and at different maturity levels in Christ.

So, what I am saying is if you want your relationship with God to grow then so must your prayer life and the things you do for God through the submission of your will. Always remember what Jesus said in
Matthew 16: 24 (TPT)
24 *"If you truly want to follow me, you should at once completely reject and disown your own life. And you must be willing to share my cross and experience it as your own,as you continually surrender to my ways."*
John 14: 15 (NLT)
15*"If you love me, obeymy commandments.*
He also said this in **John 17**
John 17: 21 (NLT)
21*I pray that they will all be one, just as you and I are one—as you are in me, Father, and I am in you. And may they be in us so that the world will believe you sent me.*
and what I discovered was that the bible was showing me through the discernment of the Holy Spirit that my relationship with Jesus was suppose, to be the same relationship He has with the Father.
I remember once I was contacted on my Facebook page set up for the Lord to support Kevin and his message by a paster out of Maryland who felt led to contact me, sending me this message.
"Is it possible for us to talk? You can check my twitter and FB page to determine if I'm worth the time to talk. I'm sensing I'm to connect with you ...but 10,000 people may feel the same way and not necessarily from the Lord. But let me know if what I'm asking is the mind of the Lord. God Bless." The man was not only a pastor but had been involved in ministry at a senior level for 38 years.
My response was this.
"Hi, this page belongs to the Lord as I am just a caretaker, but I would be glad to talk with another brother in Jesus Christ if you so feel led. A born again, Child of God is always worth the time. What do you feel is from the Lord?"

We got in contact with each other and spoke several times over the coming weeks, at first, I thought the Lord wanted me to give him a message, but after some time had passed, I began to realize the Lord had a message for both of us and He was using each other to give it. I remember after talking with him over the coming weeks about Kevin Zadai and the things going on in each other's lives, I had discovered one of the things he was dealing with was financial debt.

While driving home after work one day the Lord in a quiet voice in my heart said I want you to give him some money, I responded back ok how much? 800 dollars I thought to myself, immediately the Lord responded back and said no a thousand dollars, I want you to give him a thousand dollars. I did not know this pastor, and I was not financially a rich person, but I said OK, I will.

The next time I was to talk to the pastor I told him what the Lord had asked me to do, and then sent him the thousand dollars. The message from this I believe was to see if I would obey the Lord and detach myself from the money as I had never been asked to do this before, and the message to the pastor I believe was this is how easy it is to pay off your debt if you trust me in everything.

I also remember another story that happened to my wife who is known for being a Christian and trusting God at her workplace, without going into too much detail I will share with you an event that happened. One day she was asked by another part of management in the company she worked for to do something she not only new was wrong but was illegal as well, her response was that she could not do what they were asking of her as it would be wrong to do so, needless to say this created a lot of problems for her to the point that she almost lost her job. It was a very stressful time, but she placed her trusted in God and stood firm. I remember her saying to me that day when I came home, God found me this job and if need be, he will find me another I will do what I know to be right.

That night we both prayed and turned it over to Him saying we trust you Father, we know you've got this then we sent out the Host of Heaven in Jesus name to do battle on her behalf, to take down the enemy as well as every plot and plan that was coming against her. The following day she was asked to join a meeting where they preceded to discuss the situation and in the end God, worked it all out for the better. It was a month later she would receive a bonus of 15,000 dollars and then 2 months later, another bonus for 30,000 dollars God was paying her back for standing firm and placing all her trust in Him to work it out.

This is one more example amongst many of relationship, my wife who has a well, paying job thanks to God was willing to sacrifice it all for the truth and her relationship with Him. Again, I will say, it's just as Kevin Zadai say's you just can't make this stuff up.

Having a relationship with God means that sometimes He's going to take you outside your comfort zone, and you must be willing to walk with Him when that happens.

There is power available to all of us, but it's going to be by you losing and Him gaining.

I also discovered that through a relationship with God and a development of trust, you will have very little to no stress in your life, and that happiness as well as joy can come from nowhere. Troubles will come that's just part of living in a fallen world but how they affect you and how you deal with them will be different. My life is truly peaceful as long as I stay in Christ Jesus, for He is my peace.

Jesus has told me many times in prayer, "I have great plans for you, stay in me, and watch where I take you." To this day I do not know what those plans are. Maybe it was to write this book, I don't know. But I do know that my life is unfolding daily in a great and powerful way, and so will yours as you grow in your faith and submit your will to Him.

Chapter 6

Walking in Authority

In order to walk in authority, I first had to learn what authority was. I was never taught in the church, that after accepting Jesus as my savior, I was now on the front lines of a massive spiritual war that I could not see or feel without the guidance of the Holy Spirit. Jesus was now living through me, and that meant I had to walk in the authority I had been given through the shed blood of Christ.

So, what was walking in authority? I would listen to Jesus speak on this topic through Kevin Zadai, and would discover that it was knowing your enemy, and understanding that as a child of God, I held a position of true authority that had been returned to me. I needed to learn who the demonic were and how they operated. I needed to understand the whole picture as to how I was born into a fallen world in the first place. You see, once I understood who I was in Christ, how the enemy operated in my life and in the world, I could begin to walk in the authority that was rightfully mine.

Through Jesus I learned that not only do demons hate me, but they also use my emotions against me by way of manipulation to try to make me feel thoughts of inferiority, anger, resentment, pride, fear, etc., or to separate me from God by trying to convince me that I'm not good enough. They embed or influence thoughts that are not of God, and it is up to me as to what I choose to do with those thoughts when they come.

2 Timothy 1-7 (NLT)
7For God has not given us a spirit of fear and timidity, but of power, love, and self-discipline.
Paul said in Corinthians,
1 Corinthians 9: 24-27 (TPT)
Paul's Disciplined Lifestyle
24 Isn't it obvious that all runners on the racetrackkeep on running to win, but only one receives the victor's prize? Yet each one of you must run the race to be victorious. 25 A true athlete will be disciplined in every respect, practicing constant self-control in order to win a laurel wreath that quickly withers. But we run our race to win a victor's crown that will last forever. 26 For that reason, I don't run just for exercise or box like one throwing aimless punches, 27 but I train like a champion athlete. I subdue my body and get it under my control, so that after preaching the good news to others I myself won't be disqualified.
2 Corinthians 10: 5 (TPT)
5 We can demolish every deceptive fantasy that opposes God and break through every arrogant attitude that is raised up in defiance of the true knowledge of God. We capture, like prisoners of war, every thoughtand insist that it bow in obedience to the Anointed One.
James 1: 12-16 (TPT)
12 If your faith remains strong, even while surrounded by life's difficulties, you will continue to experience the untold blessings of God! True happiness comes as you pass the test with faith, and receive the victorious crown of life promised to every lover of God!
13 When you are tempted don't ever say, "God is tempting me," for God is incapable of being tempted by evil and he is never the source of temptation. 14 Instead it is each person's own desires and thoughts that drag them into evil and lure them away into darkness. 15 Evil desires give birth to evil actions. And when sin is fully mature it can murder you! 16 So my friends, don't be fooled by your own desires!

Through the power of the Holy Spirit, we must learn to live with perseverance, self-control, and discipline, training our bodies to discern every thought that is not of God. We capture those thoughts and pass them through without nurturing or giving life to them in any way. I found that over time with practice and guidance from the Holy Spirit that this was possible, but by no means easy.

I remember once in prayer that I asked Jesus (no, actually I pleaded with Him), to just change me in an instant, so that I could overcome these things, but the response I got back was, "That's not how it works. It's a process you must go through. Trust, stay in me, and you will overcome as I have already overcome the world."

At this point I knew that through the blood of Jesus I had the power to overcome satan and his demons.

Luke 10:19-21 (TPT)

19 Now you understand that I have imparted to you my authority to trample over his kingdom. You will trample upon every demon before you and overcome every powersatan possesses. Absolutely nothing will harm you as you walk in this authority. 20 However, your real source of joy isn't merely that these spirits submit to your authority, but that your names are written in the journals of heaven and that you belong to God's kingdom. This is the true source of your authority."

21 Then Jesus, overflowing with the Holy Spirit's joy, exclaimed, "Father, thank you, for you are Lord Supreme over heaven and earth! You have hidden the great revelation of this authority from those who are proud, those wise in their own eyes, and you have shared it with these who humbled themselves. Yes, Father. This is what pleases your heart: to give these things to those who are like trusting children.

I also knew that there were many of them throughout the world. They were those who died during the flood of Noah. Or, as Kevin puts it, "There is not just one demon behind every tree, there's five." So, though I may cast away one demon, another or even others may return in its place at a later time. When thoughts or influences come upon me again that are not of God, I need to cast those away and be aware that it may not be the one or ones I had dealt with earlier. I also needed to think about why it may have come in the first place. Did I give it access? And if so, how? Was I holding on to or entertaining thoughts I shouldn't? Was I allowing feelings that are not of God to overtake me? Therefore, praying in tongues, having a personal relationship with God, and knowing scriptures like Psalms 91, Ephesians 6:10-18, etc. are so important, as I can use these things in my spiritual battles with evil. You need this kind of knowledge so that you do not think that you are ineffective. You need to understand the truth about what is going on around you because once you do, you can begin to take control through the blood of Christ, walking in the authority that is rightfully yours. Casting away demons here and there as well as learning to control your thoughts through the submission of your will to Jesus doesn't end the battles; it just helps you to win them when they come. The good news is the devil will flee from you over time if you are persistent and you learn to overcome yourself and trust in Christ. Learning to come to the end of yourself is a very important step in your relationship with God.

Ephesians 6:10-18 (TPT)

Spiritual Warfare

10 Now my beloved ones, I have saved these most important truths for last: Be supernaturally infused with strength through your life-union with the Lord Jesus. Stand victorious with the force of his explosive power flowing in and through you.

11 Put on God's complete set of armor provided for us, so that you will be protected as you fight against the evil strategies of the accuser! 12 Your hand-to-hand combat is not with human beings, but with the highest principalities and authorities operating in rebellion under the heavenly realms. For they are a powerful class of demon-gods and evil spirits that hold this dark world in bondage. 13 Because of this, you must wear all the

armor that God provides so you're protected as you confront the slanderer, for you are destined for all things and will rise victorious.
14 Put on truth as a belt to strengthen you to stand in triumph. Put on holiness as the protective armor that covers your heart. 15 Stand on your feet alert, then you'll always be ready to share the blessings of peace.
16 In every battle, take faith as your wrap-around shield, for it is able to extinguish the blazing arrows coming at you from the Evil One! 17-18 Embrace the power of salvation's full deliverance, like a helmet to protect your thoughts from lies. And take the mighty razor-sharp Spirit-sword of the spoken Word of God. Pray passionately in the Spirit, as you constantly intercede with every form of prayer at all times. Pray the blessings of God upon all his believers.

You see, just by reading Ephesians 6:10-18 you learn a lot about your enemy, as in every protection of God's armor is an opposite, that is there to attack you. These are some of the things that will help you to better understand your enemy, and if you apply them to your life, they will make you more effective.

It's like Kevin says, you do not fight the devil on his ground and on his terms. You make him come to you and let the Lord fight for you through the obedience and the submission of your will.

I would also come to know that demons are territorial and that what comes against me in one city or state is different than what comes against me in another. Again, good things to know as you begin to walk in authority. I would always remember what is says in 1 John 4.

1 John 4: 4 (TPT)

4 Little Children, you can be certain that you belong to God and have Conquered them, for the One who is living in you is far greater than the one who is in the world.

The good news was that I knew over time I would be successful and that they would eventually flee from me if I was persistent. Of course, I also had to remain persistent in the other areas of my life as well.

James 4: 7 (TPT)

7 So then, surrender to God. Stand up to the devil and resist him and he will turn and run away from you.

You also need to know that once they flee from you, they may try to enter or influence someone close to you, like a friend or a family member. I found that it was important to pray for these people every day and to always be aware of what's going on around you, so that you can see these things and deal with them correctly. Knowledge is the key, and your power lies in Jesus Christ.

It was my prayers to God through Jesus Christ for deeper understanding that would aid me in my walk. I wanted to know so many things, but I needed to know the truth, as it was the truth that would set me free. So many churches only teach the surface of the scriptures, and it wasn't until Jesus led me to Kevin Zadai that I began to truly understand many things. I also knew that my discernment or understanding needed to come from the Holy Spirit and not me or the world. I knew that God would never deny truth from a child who truly wanted it as long as they came to Him in humility with a pure, contrite heart.

You see, many people want the truth, but do they really want it or are they looking for God to side with them and what they have already determined the truth to be? This is the defining difference. So, again I knew that if I truly wanted truth that I would have to come to God with a pure and contrite heart. I would pray to God humbly in humility and say, "I don't know the truth, but through my great teacher the Holy Spirit I can be shown the truth and have my eyes opened." This is how I would go about gaining truth—praying to the Holy Spirit to open my eyes so that I can understand what I am hearing, reading, or seeing.

1 Corinthians 2:14-16 (TPT)

14 Someone living on an entirely human levelrejectsthe revelations of God's Spirit, for they make no sense to him. He can't understand the revelations of the Spirit because they are only discovered by the illumination of the Spirit. 15 Those who live in the Spirit are able to carefully evaluate all things, and they are subject to the scrutiny of no one but God. 16 For Who has ever intimately known the mind of the Lord Yahweh well enough to become his counselor?

1 Corinthians 2:11 (TPT)

11 After all, who can really see into a person's heart and know his hidden impulses except for that person's spirit? So, it is with God. His thoughts and secrets are only fully understood by his Spirit, the Spirit of God.

In my walk and relationship with God, I believe that one of the most important things I have learned is the importance in the ability to humble myself. It's not easy, but if you want to mature in Christ, humility will be one of the most important traits you can add to yourself, for with humility will come great strength and understanding. Never fool yourself into thinking that God does not know your true intentions, as He knows you better than you know yourself. Make sure when you come to Him for truth, it's the truth you really seek.

Romans 8: 27 (TPT)

Living by the Power of the Holy Spirit

27 God, the searcher of the heart, knows fully our longings, yet he also understands the desires of the Spirit, because the Holy Spirit passionately pleads before God for us, his holy ones, in perfect harmony with God's plan and our destiny.

Proverbs 11: 2 (TPT)

2 When you act with presumption, convinced that you're right, don't be surprised if you fall flat on your face! But walking in humility helps you to make wise decisions.

In conclusion, Jesus didn't just buy my salvation so that I could live a better life and wait for Him to come back. If that were the case, He would have taken me to heaven the minute I chose to believe and accept Him as my Savior. He died for me and brought my spirit back to the state of Adam, even higher, so that I could walk in authority on this earth while letting Him live through me by way of the submission of my will. Letting Jesus live through me would mean that I would begin to mature in the spirit, to act like Him, walk like Him, and do the things that He did. The scriptures say even greater things. So, what did Jesus do when He walked on the earth?

He walked in authority, and Matthew 4 tells us the rest.

Matthew 4: 23-24(TPT)

Jesus' Ministry of Healing

23 Jesus ministered from place to place throughout all of the province of Galilee. He taught in the synagogues, preaching the hope of the kingdom realm and healing every kind of sickness and disease among the people. 24 His fame spread everywhere! Many people who were in pain and suffering with every kind of illness were brought to Jesus for their healing—epileptics, paralytics, and those tormented by demonic powers were all set free. Everyone who was brought to Jesus was healed!

This is how I, and others, are supposed to live our lives while we wait for our King to come back. We live in the world, but we are not of the world.

Knowing who I am in Christ is a very important step in my walk so that I can, (through the maturity of my spirit) become a beacon to others to discover who they are as well.

Romans 8: 29 (TPT)

29 For he knew all about us before we were born and he destined us from the beginning to share the likeness of his Son. This means the Son is the oldest among a vast family of brothers and sisters who will become just like him.

Walking in authority requires maturity in the spirit. Maturity in the spirit requires submission of your will. Submission of your will allows Jesus to live through you. Jesus living through you allows you to walk in authority.

Chapter 7

Discerning Favor in Your Life

In order to experience the favor of God in my life, I had to first come to understand how to recognize it. Many Christians have more favor in their lives than they realize but have not learned how to see it. A good percentage of them attribute favor with money, and though this may be part of it, in my experiences I have learned that favor comes in many ways.

It is important to be able to see favor in your life. One, because it helps in strengthening your faith but most importantly it allows you to thank God for everything He does, small or large. We all know how it feels when we do something good for our children and they don't recognize it. So how much more important is it to recognize all the good things our Father does for us?

Luke 11: 11-13 (TPT)

11 "Let me ask you this: Do you know of any father who would give his son a snake on a plate when he asked for a serving of fish? Of course not! 12 Do you know of any father who would give his daughter a spider when she had asked for an egg? Of course not!13 If imperfect parents know how to lovingly take care of their children and give them what they need, how much more will the perfect heavenly Father give the Holy Spirit's fullness when his children ask him."

What I learned through the deeper teachings of Jesus and the scriptures was that God already wanted to give me the desires of my heart. Rather than focus on what I thought I needed, I would transfer my focus to just wanting to know Him better. I wanted a deeper relationship, and I wanted to grow in my faith in every area of my life so that the relationship I was seeking could blossom and flourish.

I wanted to know how to please God, and everything I was discovering led back to faith. I'm not just talking about the belief that God exists and the faith that Jesus Christ is your savior, and the only way. I'm talking about complete faith in everything, faith in who you are in Christ, faith in your finances, faith in your health, faith in your joy, and happiness and faith in God through Jesus Christ to supply every need you will ever have in this life. To trust God in everything and believe that every prayer you have is answered, even if it's not according to your plans or timeline. That's what faith is or has become to me at least. Trusting in my Heavenly Father to provide all my needs.

A baby at birth can do nothing on its own, it relies on its parent to provide its every need. Just as Jesus said in Matthew 6:26-34.

Matthew 6:26-28 (TPT)

26 "Look at all the birds—do you think they worry about their existence? They don't plant or reap or store up food, yet your heavenly Father provides them each with food. Aren't you much more valuable to your Father than they? 27 So, which one of you by worrying could add anything to your life? 28 "And why would you worry about your clothing? Look at all the beautiful flowers of the field. They don't work or toil,

29 And yet not even Solomon in all his splendor was robed in beauty more than one of these! 30 So if God has clothed the meadow with hay, which is here for such a short time and then dried up and burned, won't he provide for you the clothes you need—even though you live with such little faith?

31 "So then, forsake your worries! Why would you say, 'What will we eat?' or 'What will we drink?' or 'What will we wear?' 32 For that is what the unbelievers chase after. Doesn't your heavenly Father already know the things your bodies require?

33 "So above all, constantly chase after the realm of God's kingdom and the righteousness that proceeds from him. Then all these less important things will be given to you abundantly. 34 Refuse to worry about tomorrow, but deal with each challenge that comes your way, one day at a time. Tomorrow will take care of itself."

We expect instant results in our life. I have learned that we live in a fallen world amongst an unseen spiritual war constantly going on around us. God is present in the world, but He currently allows satan to influence and control some parts of it, so things don't always happen according to our plans. But does that mean that God did not hear or answer our prayers? No!

Daniel 10 (NLT)

Daniel's Vision of a Messenger

11 And the man said to me, "Daniel, you are very precious to God, so listen carefully to what I have to say to you. Stand up, for I have been sent to you." When he said this to me, I stood up, still trembling. 12 Then he said, "Don't be afraid, Daniel. Since the first day you began to pray for understanding and to humble yourself before your God, your request has been heard in heaven. I have come in answer to your prayer. 13 But for twenty-one days the spirit princeof the kingdom of Persia blocked my way. Then Michael, one of the archangels, came to help me, and I left him there with the spirit prince of the kingdom of Persia.14 Now I am here to explain what will happen to your people in the future, for this vision concerns a time yet to come."

These are the things we need to understand to mature in our faith. It was important for me to be aware of the deeper truths of the scriptures in order to discern the favor I have, and to continue to receive it from God.

I was aware of who I was in Christ, that my Heavenly Father loved me more than I could ever know, and yes, that I was born into a fallen world that did not operate the way God had originally designed it to be. This was the truth. If I was to discern the favor in my life, I had to be aware of who I really was and the world I was living in.

So, what did I discover favor to be? Favor was everything. All the things that were present in my life—my health, my family and their salvation, my friends, my job, my finances, my good fortune, my discernment, my opportunities to do God's work because I was trusted.

I also discovered that the less I pursued or chased things and the more I became a good receiver by allowing God to work through me, the more favor He would impart.

I would thank God every day for all the things that He did in my life, and I would also thank Him for and acknowledge every material item that I had in my possession, letting Him know that I was aware that it had come from Him, and I was truly grateful. I even thanked Him for the opportunities He had brought my way to talk about Jesus and who we truly are in Christ. He gave me numerous opportunities to share about Kevin Zadai with many people. Yes, Jesus had taught me many things through Kevin Zadai. My wife and I have been truly blessed because of it.

I considered it an honor every time God created an opportunity for me to share something or help someone, as I knew that these things had come my way because God trusted me. I was building a relationship with Him, and in the process learning through the gift of the Holy Spirit to not only understand but discern the favor He was giving to me. The more spiritually mature you become, the more you are able to see, which will only make your faith stronger.

I realized that in discerning favor I could recognize the many gifts that God had given me. You discern everything. Every day you are given the very air you breathe—it's all a gift. Creation is a gift, being made out of the likeness of God is a gift, understanding and patience is a gift, health, prosperity, your faith is a gift. Knowing God's hand is in your circumstances when it's not always easy to see (or in some cases where time needs to pass), can be seen as a gift. Being used as a vessel for God's purpose is a gift, and the salvation given through Jesus Christ is the greatest gift of all.

Chapter 8

The Book of Miracles

After I had made the commitment to Jesus – as mentioned in chapter five of this book – to apply all that I was learning from Him through Kevin Zadai, many things happened. Things like coming to the end of myself, finding where I end and where Jesus begins, tithing my time and income, taking the rightful authority back in my life that Jesus had given me through His blood and turning it on the devil, praying in tongues throughout my day (usually one to two hours), changing nearly all of my prayer life to prayers for other people (and when I did pray for myself or my wife, it was in most cases to have a closer relationship with God). I would take time in my prayer life where I did not ask God for anything but to just experience the Father's and Jesus' presence in meditative prayer, sometimes to music by the Riveras or Kevin Zadai. I was learning to share the word and to see the opportunities that my angels or the Holy Spirit provided for me. I was giving to the homeless or people in need with a happy heart. I was asking the Holy Spirit for discernment and reading the word almost every day. I was taking back control of my mind by listening to the teaching of the Holy Spirit on how to take every thought that was not of God into captivity and pass it through rather than nurturing and bringing it to life. I was creating a state in my life of constantly seeking God at every turn. I was trusting God in everything and doing what Jesus had asked me to do years ago, to listen to and support Kevin Zadai in everything he did.

These were just some of the things I began to do in my life as I continued to learn more from His teachings – the list as well as my learning continues to grow to this day. I tell you these things because I can only use my life as an example of what happened to me and my wife when we started to apply the things we were learning. Yes, favor began to appear, and in some cases, it came in very unusual ways.

After about a year or so, my wife and I decided to create a book of miracles because so many things were happening to us, and we did not want to forget any of them. If I remember correctly, we are at forty miracles over the course of three and a half years. Yes, it was pretty amazing. I will not share all forty, but I will share a few of the biggest ones from our book.

I will start with the sale of our house back in California. My wife and I were talking about possibly selling our house and renting for a while, as we felt the market was going to head in a bad direction in the near future. I had been a real-estate agent in the past and had a current license but was not working in the real estate industry at that time. We began to look at different houses that had sold in the area so that I could assess the value of our house. Then we started talking about getting an agent.

It was not long after I was told in prayer that if my faith was to grow, I would need to leave the area, not just to another city, but I would have to move to a different state and leave everything behind. I sat down one night and shared this information with my wife. We had spent our entire lives in California, she had a career of twenty-four years at a law firm and I had a degree in Film and a career in sales for the last seven – this was no minor conversation. At the time we already had some family who had moved to the state of Washington, but we also still had many family members and friends living in California. We discussed it for a while and decided that obeying the Lord and moving would be the wisest choice.

After finding an agent and going back and forth on the price, we listed the house. The agent thought that the price I wanted to list the house for was too high. We decided against his advice and told him to try it, but if we didn't get any bites, he said we would need to be prepared to lower it. One hour after we listed the house it sold. Not only did it sell, but it sold for over $5,000 more than the listing price. The agent said it was the fastest sale of a house he had ever done.

What I want you to remember is that I never asked the Lord to sell our house. Even after He told me that I needed to leave the area, I just did what He asked me to do, which was to sell the house and move to another state. In return, because we obeyed Him, our house sold in one hour and for $5,000 more than the listing price. Did I mention that it was also a Christian couple who bought it?

The second miracle that I will share with you happened after we sold our house in California. We had been listening to Jesus speak through Kevin Zadai for over two and a half years. I had mentioned to my wife on several occasions that I felt it would be necessary for us to see Kevin Zadai in person, before the first part of his ministry ended – which would be at the three-year mark. But he was never in an area close to us; he was usually speaking closer to the east coast or in the Southwest states like Arizona.

One day my wife called and told me that Kevin Zadai was going to be in Illinois at River Destiny Church. It was going to be one of his last speaking engagements before his three-year mark ended. The important thing to note here was that the Lord had told me in prayer to pay off all our debt. We had paid off everything except our house and going on this trip, we would have to charge it. After our flights and a hotel, the total came out to be about $2,600. I prayed about it that night, and the Lord said to me in prayer, "I bid you to come," so I told my wife to book the trip, and that we would pay it off as soon as we could. The very next day my wife called me in tears saying, "You won't believe what just happened. My boss texted me and told me to give myself a $5,000 bonus." My wife is the one who takes care of all the accounting in the office, so our trip just got paid for. We could now pay off our credit card.

What I want you to remember again is that I never asked the Lord to pay for our trip. I just did what I knew He wanted us to do, which was to come to hear Him speak at River Destiny Church in Lostant, Illinois. Not only did He pay off the trip, but we had money to spare.

There was one other thing that happened to me while on this trip. We were there for three days, and on the second day I had a gift I wanted to give to Kevin and Kathi Zadai. It was extremely hard to get any personal time to talk to Kevin, and so that morning in our hotel room I asked the Lord to help me get a chance to meet him. The Lord responded, "I will provide a way today for you to meet Kevin." They were holding the meeting in the Lostant school gym because more people had shown up than they had expected, and they needed extra room.

I remember walking in with my wife, and saying to myself, "OK Lord, how am I going to meet him?" After my wife and I sat down in our chairs, I decided to walk around for a bit. Long high curtains had been hung across the end of the gymnasium to provide an area where the crew could walk around unseen. Shortly after I had gotten up, I heard someone banging on one of the back doors of the gymnasium. I walked to the curtain and peeked my head through one of the openings. Through the glass windows of the gymnasium doors and to my amazement stood Kevin Zadai, his wife Kathi, and their bodyguard. They had been locked out. I hurried to the door and let them in. I immediately tried to start a conversation with Kevin, but all he said to me was, "God bless you," and then walked into a back room as his bodyguard blocked me from him. I was very hurt but before I could say a word, the Holy Spirit came over me and said, "Don't say anything.

Just trust." I returned to my seat beside my wife, still hurt because I had come such a long way, and I just wanted a brief moment of his time to show him something that I wanted to give him.

I sat for a short while but was too stressed to just sit. It wasn't long before I got up again to walk around some more. I walked over to the table where Kevin sells all his books, CDs, etc., and I saw his wife, Kathi. When I approached her, she said to me, "We are sorry about that, but Kevin has to listen to the Lord's instructions before he speaks, and it gets very intense for him." I responded that it was OK, and that I understood. I proceeded to show her what I wanted to show him – I had a gift for Kevin of which I am unable to disclose the details of in this book. She then asked, "Could you send that to me? I will show it to him when I get a chance". And so, I did. About a week later I received a message saying that she had shown Kevin what I had given to her, and he really liked it.

I was very happy at this point. Not just because I was successful in giving something to someone, I had great respect for, but because the Lord had done all He said He would do, and I was amazed at how He had worked out everything because I had trusted Him and remained patient. On a side note – the worship service they held there was the most amazing service we had ever experienced. My wife and I were almost certain that we heard angels singing along with the group.

The third miracle I will share with you regards our recently purchased home in Washington. The house was on a city sewage system, but unbeknownst to us, we still had a septic pump that went into a 100-gallon tank, which was then pumped up the hill to the city system. It was a weird setup but was necessary based on the location of the house in relation to the city line.

One day I heard a loud alarm sound coming from the porch of our house. When I went to check it out, I discovered we had a small tank with a pump, and the alarm going off was because the pump was not functioning. Well, under the home warranty, someone came to look at it, and we were told that it would cost over $10,000 to fix as the pumps were very expensive. So, we both prayed to God and said, "We know you've got this, and we trust that you will find a way to make this work out for the good." God knew we did not have the money for this, but we never lost hope. After turning in the claim, it was deemed to be a non-covered item. Even though it was not a full septic system, it was not a regular system either and therefore they would not cover it.

We spoke with the technician who came out to look at it. He said that he would cut us a deal and fix it on the side through his company for $6,500. He could buy the pump through his company for less. Unfortunately, we still did not have that kind of money, so we decided to send the claim to our homeowners' insurance. I also spoke with an electrician who had come out to see if the problem was electrical, and sadly enough it was not. After talking with him a bit, I came to discover that he too was a Christian. He told me he knew of an electric motor company in town that might be able to fix it for a lot less, so he gave me the contact and helped me pull the pump to take it over.

After a short time, our homeowner's insurance company called us and said that they would not cover the pump as it was not a covered item in their policy, so we were back to square one. We then decided to call the real estate agent that represented us in the purchase of the home to talk to him about the home warranty and to see if he could help us in any way (as we were never told about this type of system being part of the house when we purchased it). He said that he knew the head guy at the home warranty company and would see what he could do.

Later that week I would hear back from our real estate agent who told us that he was able to get the pump covered after providing additional documentation, however, they were only going to give us $500. Shortly after this, I received a call from the guy at the electric motor company who the Christian electrician had referred me to. The man said to me, "Hey, I was working on your pump, and it just started working, so I'm going to lube up all the internal parts and you can come get it tomorrow. The cost will just be one hundred dollars." My wife and I were ecstatic, so I called the electrician who had referred the shop to me to let him know the good news. He said he would come out the next day to hook up the electrical and to help me reinstall it. He said the cost would be $200 – and yes, you guessed it – we ended up with $200 in our pocket after all was said and done. Glory be to God. Our trust and patience had paid off. In the end the broken septic pump job with a cost of $10,000 to fix three weeks later, miraculously turned into a $300 job. Take note again that we never asked the Lord to fix the pump. All we said was, "Lord we trust you, and we know you will make this work out for the best."

The fourth miracle I will share with you was when my wife and I obeyed the Lord in moving to Washington State. We had chosen this state because it was the only other state where we had family. I remember the long drive from California on the day we moved. We were three-quarters of the way there going over a mountain pass when the transmission in the U-Haul van began to give out. The U-Haul would not go over a speed of 45MPH and if it had broken down at that time, we would have been in a world of hurt, but God made sure that it lasted just long enough to get us there. He was with us and I felt it. Glory be to God!

The fifth Miracle was when my wife left her law firm job that she had resided at for twenty-four years, and I left a seven-year job. But by the grace of God, I had already lined up a job before we left. My wife, however, was still looking. Several months would go by as she continued to work with different temp agencies. Opportunities would arise, but nothing would pan out. She would post her resumé on different job websites, waiting to hear back. We never lost hope and knew that God would provide a way if we just kept trusting in our faith. One day my wife got a call from a temp agency that she was not signed up with. They had found her resumé online and wanted to see if she could come in to interview for a controller position in a multimillion-dollar manufacturing company, so she agreed and went. After the interview, they agreed to hire her as a temp, as they usually did not hire people until they had been working for the company for at least two years.

I remember my wife's frustration with this job as there was much to learn and very little time to learn it. She was replacing a woman who had been with the company for many years and would be retiring soon due to arising health issues. There were several people who had come in for this job before my wife, and quit shortly after, so the woman she was to replace was really hoping my wife would stick it out. As I said earlier, there was a lot to learn in a very short time, and my wife almost quit on more than one occasion. The reason she did not would surprise you, as she felt an obligation to the woman, she would be replacing who we learned was sick with cancer. I remember her telling me, "I want to quit, but I just can't do it to this woman, she needs me." So, she prayed to God to help her.

Here is where it gets good. Because my wife trusted God and stayed in there, not for herself but for another person she wanted to help, a person who really needed her to stay so that she could retire, she was rewarded. That week not only did they waive the two-year working requirement to be hired on with the company, but they offered her a salary that was almost twice as much as what she was being paid before at her previous law firm of twenty-four years. My wife took over the job, and with her trust in God, found ways to not only teach herself the things she needed to know, but also to create ways to make a complex job easier. Sadly, the woman who retired, passed a year later. In the end, God not only rewarded my wife with a much better paying job but also gave her the wisdom and strength to trust that He could help her learn what she needed to know to be successful.

The sixth miracle I will share with you is when I started a new job in Vancouver, Washington, in order to be closer to my church. I was told when I started the job that there was a bonus, I would receive every

November of about $5,000 to $7,000. The only catch was that I was required to have started my employment there before a certain date in order to collect it, and because I was starting this job in March it would be almost one and a half years before that time would come. The owner of this company was very frugal with his money and made no exceptions.

One day at work in the middle of November, my boss pulled me aside to tell me, "Hey, it looks like that bonus you were supposed to get next year is going to be given to you this year. Yep, they're giving you a $5,000 check in a couple of days." I never asked God to do this. It just happened.

The seventh and final miracle I will share with you was when the COVID-19 virus hit. I was watching Sid Roth that week. He was talking about what people should be doing during the pandemic. One of the things he said was to use this time to get closer to God, to pray against the virus, and to take communion every night as well as read Psalms 91. My wife and I did just that. We would recite the Lord's prayer, pray against evil and for God's will to be done through the president, as well as for his safety and protection. Then we would pray against the virus, take communion, and finish it up with the Psalms 91 prayer provided online by Sid Roth. During this time, I not only continued to tithe my 10 percent but also gave more of my personal time to God, and in doing so almost completed this book. We trusted God and asked Him for nothing other than to watch over us and our family. We worried about nothing, and the people around us knew it. I asked several people I knew if they were in need of anything. We never even wore a mask except when we went out and it was required to go into a store, a place of business, or in certain circumstances at our work. I remembered what Jesus had said in Matthew 17:27, when He was asked to pay a tax.

Matthew 17:27 (TPT)

27 But, so that we don't offend them, go to the lake and throw out your hook, and the first fish that rises up will have a coin in its mouth. It will be the exact amount you need to pay the temple tax for both of us."

Over the course of the next four months, I was laid off for two months; during that time, I received more money than I had been making at work full-time. After going back to work, I received two bonuses and my wife received one from her work as well. We made more money in those four months than we had made in any four months of that current year. As Kevin once put it, you will sow in famine and reap a hundredfold. The lesson for me in this miracle was at a time of intense stress for many in our nation. My wife and I trusted God to not only protect us but to meet our needs as we continued to give and operate as though nothing was going on.

These are just a few of mine as well as my wife's experiences written in our book of miracles. I share them with a humble heart knowing that you can have even greater.

Additionally, my wife and I have made a great effort over the years to stay balanced with God in all our ways. We go to church, we belong to a Bible study group, we tithe our income and our time to do the Lord's work. We pray and read the Bible regularly, we pray in tongues often, and we make time to pray privately together or alone, seeking personal time with God where we ask for nothing but relationship and the presence of the Father and the Son.

I'm not saying we are perfect, in fact far from it, but my wife and I seek God diligently, and we trust Him.

Every individual is on their own personal walk with God. We are all growing in Christ and at different levels of maturity. I believe what we should look for in our lives is whether we are continually moving forward in Jesus Christ.

I remember Kevin telling a story once about when he was with Jesus in heaven and that Jesus had told him that he was well-known and talked about there. Jesus had also told Kevin that he had done everything

that He had ever asked him to do, and that was rare on the Earth. I remember once in prayer I asked the Lord about this. I had asked Him to explain to me how Kevin had done everything He had asked him to do. His response to me was, "Kevin lives from his heart, he listens, and makes his choices from there."
Because of Jesus and the gift of the Holy Spirit, my wife and I continually learn more each day, knowing that the more we learn and apply to our lives, the better understanding and closer relationship with God we will have.

Chapter 9

My New Life in Christ

What is a new life? A new life is change, the beginning of something new, a feeling deep inside you that you can't explain but it tells you that you're more than this, it says I know you, I know you better than you know yourself, so trust in me and let me show you who you really are. That's it, when your journey with Jesus Christ begins and your life with the world comes to an end. It's when Jesus begins to reveal to you all truth, the truth of who you are in Him, how much He truly loves you, and how unique and special you really are. It is a truth so good you can barely wrap your mind around it, but it's true, because in your spirit you can feel it as Jesus pulls away the veil and reveals to you the truth the world has hidden from you for so long.

It's been almost four years since I began this journey of truth, and I am not the same person I was when it started. Though my journey with Jesus is ongoing, my life has become a better place, filled with truth, understanding, and an inner peace I can't explain. The fears and worries I used to have are gone, and I can now see, as well as feel, God's presence in my life. My understanding and maturity in the spirit grows by the day through God's word and prayer. I am still me, but I'm different, and the world around me is different as well. My spirit is now a magnet that is drawn to God, as Jesus has paved my way back to the Father through His precious blood.

I am learning what it means to be a child of God, and to walk in the authority that is rightfully mine through the shed blood of Jesus Christ my King. My purpose in life now is to live by faith and to work in unity with my angels and the Holy Spirit. It is essential that through the submission of my will I come to the end of myself, for it is only there that Jesus will be able to give to me all that He has in store for my life. I must learn to use the gifts that He gave to me at the moment of my creation by praying in the spirit and through the opening of my books in heaven. It will be Jesus living through me that will allow me to complete my journey in Him.

Now that I am awake through the discernment of the Holy Spirit and the submission of my will, the world has become a different place just as I have become a different person. Life here to me is no longer real in the sense that it's only a remnant or shadow of what God had originally made. I am only a visitor here now, a visitor living in a fallen world, and there is much to do while I am still here.

This relationship with God building inside me, changing me by the day, has brought me great peace, but with that said, it has also brought me more understanding and awareness of the great spiritual battle that wages in the world and inside myself. Now that I am aware that there are outside influences that I cannot see manipulating myself and the world around me, I must remember to always walk in the authority that Jesus Christ suffered and died for.

As my relationship with Jesus grows, so does the battle that wages inside myself. This is where I have learned that even though I have been redeemed by the blood of Christ, I still must rely on Him to fight this battle for me by submitting to Him and using the authority He gave back to me. Turning the tides on evil, and knowing that it will eventually flee from me, requires an understanding of who I am in Christ. As I stated earlier in chapter six of this book, without Jesus I can do nothing.

James 4 (TPT)

Living Close to God

7 So then, surrender to God. Stand up to the devil and resist him and he will turn and run away from you. 8 Move your heart closer and closer to God, and he will come even closer to you. But make sure you cleanse your life, you sinners, and keep your heart pure and stop doubting. 9 Feel the pain of your sin, be sorrowful and weep! Let your joking around be turned into mourning and your joy into deep humiliation. 10 Be willing to be made low before the Lord and he will exalt you!

John 15 (TPT)

Jesus the Living Vine

5 "I am the sprouting vine and you're my branches. As you live in union with me as your source, fruitfulness will stream from within you—but when you live separated from me you are powerless. 6 If a person is separated from me, he is discarded; such branches are gathered up and thrown into the fire to be burned. 7 But if you live in life-union with me and if my words live powerfully within you—then you can ask whatever you desire and it will be done. 8 When your lives bear abundant fruit, you demonstrate that you are my mature disciples who glorify my Father! 9 "I love each of you with the same love that the Father loves me. You must continually let my love nourish your hearts. 10 If you keep my commands, you will live in my love, just as I have kept my Father's commands, for I continually live nourished and empowered by his love. 11 My purpose for telling you these things is so that the joy that I experience will fill your hearts with overflowing gladness! 12 "So this is my command: Love each other deeply, as much as I have loved you. 13 For the greatest love of all is a love that sacrifices all. And this great love is demonstrated when a person sacrifices his life for his friends."

I have learned to pray with a deeper spiritual love toward God, and I am so glad that Jesus brought me unto Himself through Kevin Zadai. Kevin is the beginning of the next move of God. Jesus told me recently after praying in tongues for an hour, that Kevin is the bridge that I've put in place to bring people unto myself. Everyone needs to know of him and share him everywhere. I believe this message was given to me because normally I share Kevin with everyone I can. Recently I worked with a husband and wife who, through conversation I had discovered were Christians, but I realized I had forgotten to share Kevin with them before they left, even though the opportunity was presented. I believe the message was to remind me of how important it is to not only be aware but to take advantage of every opportunity that the Lord sends my way.

It is important as you mature in Christ to always be aware of what God is doing around you. It is so easy to miss an opportunity to assist in opening someone's world to a deeper understanding and stronger relationship with Jesus, or maybe just a relationship in general. Operating in God's will, requires submission and awareness of spirit.

With the above said, here is an example of when I was operating in God's will. Once while I was working with a customer from out of town, I discovered that she was a Christian. She had kind of drifted away from her faith after her mother, who was a devout Christian and a firm believer in healing, had passed away. I remember her telling me that she had drifted away from her faith because God did not heal her mother. We talked about this for a while and then I asked her, "When God did not heal your mother, did her faith fall away?" She responded and said, "No, in fact even though she had Alzheimer's, they would still catch her from time to time praying in tongues, but she never fell away, even up to the end."

I explained to her that God is not the cause of sickness in this world, satan is. Depending on the spiritual maturity of the person, God may use them to reach others. I told her that I truly believed that her mother was probably an example of this. I told her about Kevin Zadai, a person I had been watching for years who had died, gone to Heaven, and was sent back by Jesus with a message.

I gave her a link to some of his videos and explained to her that Jesus had sent Kevin back with a message to help Christians in this season to better understand the scriptures and what was really going on around us. He also told Kevin that if he came back, he couldn't lose, as Jesus said He would be at his right side telling him everything He wanted him to say. I told her if you watch him, Jesus will speak to your spirit and give you a better understanding of your spiritual life, who you are in Christ, and how to live correctly in this world. You will learn things that will amaze you and fill your heart with joy.

Many months later I would hear from her again, and this is what she said to me in a text:

"Thank you! I watch Kevin Zadai a lot, and have purchased several books, and one of his Warrior Notes School Courses. I have learned so much and have also relearned things I already knew. You were a godsend, and I thank God you were there, and that you were bold in witnessing to me. I would love it if you would agree with me, that God would send me a friend who believes in God the way we do, with whom I can study with. A threefold cord is not easily broken. Thank you so much." It is stories like this that let you know that you're making a difference. It was very humbling and even brought a tear to my eye.

This is why it is so important to always listen and watch for the opportunities the Holy Spirit and angels bring your way. As your relationship with God grows in maturity, you will be used more often to help other people get on track with their destiny in Christ, and you must be aware of this. As I grow spiritually, the angels trust in me to share with people as they make opportunities available. I must try to never grieve them but to let them know that they can count on me to do my part, however small it may be.

I will also say truthfully that the hardest thing for me in my walk has been coming to the end of myself. I have pleaded with God to help me in this, knowing that without Jesus I can do nothing, but with Him I can do all things. What I got back in prayer was, "I have given you the Holy Spirit, so use Him, He will guide you in truth and instruct you in everything."

I have learned in my growing relationship with Jesus that you must work in every area of your life, not just one. There must be a balance as you grow spiritually, continually moving forward in your faith. The more mature you become, the humbler you must be if your relationship is to grow. This is what I see in Kevin Zadai, and why I believe Jesus is using him as a vessel – his faith is strong, and his humbleness is amazing.

This is what I think many leaders in the church are lacking in this season, but I do believe all of this is about to change. Like I said earlier, what I have learned in my experience is that coming to the end of yourself is an absolute must for God to truly work through you. What I am saying is, as you grow in Christ and God begins to work through you more, your humbleness must grow as well or one day you may find that you are working by yourself, as I believe many are doing today.

The first word I was ever given was to a pastor in my church. I was instructed on how I was to give the word, and it was to be given in private. When I called the church, I set up an appointment to meet with the pastor. Later that week it was canceled, and his receptionist had said that the pastor had requested that I leave the word with her. I would not. Hurt by this, I shared this information with my wife and that night in prayer I asked Jesus, "What should I do?" His response was, "Nothing, I will go to him tonight."

The next day my wife called me. She said the pastor had put up a video on how to hear God speak. I was shocked, so I had my wife send me the link and I watched it. To my amazement everything the pastor said was true. When the video was done, I started to post something saying that hearing God also requires humility, and a person who is not humble can easily miss what God has to say, but the Lord told me, "Do not post anything on this video." So, I did not.

That night in prayer, Jesus said to me, "I asked you to give a word to the pastor, so why do you feel hurt because it was not well received? This is not about you, and how you feel, it's about you doing what I've asked you to do." Then He said to me, "Everything the pastor said was correct but sometimes you can get so focused on the message that you forget how to listen."

It would be months before I was permitted to go to that pastor again to share the message. This time I went to him in person. I saw him after a service one day and I reminded the pastor about the word that I had been given for him, and the appointment that I had made months earlier to meet with him that had been canceled shortly thereafter. The following day I reminded him about the message he had previously posted on 'how to hear God speak'. After hearing this he asked me, "Can you just give the message to me now, right here?" My response to him was, "No". I then relayed to him the message the Lord had given me, "what I can tell you is that later that night in prayer the Lord told me that the message you gave on hearing God speak was correct, but He also told me that sometimes you can get so focused on the message that you forget how to listen." I then told him, "I have your word, and your receptionist has my number to call me when you're ready to hear it." I never received a call from the pastor after that day and I no longer belong to that church. A year later the covid virus hit and the church began to walk in fear. It was time for me to move on, so when I found myself outside the church, I followed God to a new one where there were no masks, and the Holy Spirit was everywhere. This new church was growing at a rapid pace and was the first church I had ever been a part of where I could feel the presence of God just as I did when praying in private in my own home.

I tell this story to illustrate some of the things that I needed to learn and am still learning as my relationship with God continues to grow. It's not about me and it never will be, it's about what Jesus can do through me. The more trust He places in me, and the more spiritually mature I become, the humbler I need to be.

1 Peter 5:6 (TPT)

Humility and Faith

6 If you bow low in God's awesome presence, he will eventually exalt you as you leave the timing in his hands.

Matthew 18:4 (TPT)

4 Whoever continually humbles himself to become like this gentle child is the greatest one in heaven's kingdom realm.

God works in our lives in so many ways, and I have found that it is very important to always be aware that not everything that God does in our lives is financial. Finances are only a small part of the relationship; God supplies my needs according to what I need. It could be financial, discernment of the world, the word when I read it, or even situations in my life that need to be addressed for whatever reason. It's a relationship with God where He helps me with everything and uses me in many things depending on how strong that relationship has become, and how much He can trust me to do His will. Every day is something new, and I need to be able to see what God has in store for me as the day unfolds. This comes through knowing Him and how He works in my life.

The stronger my relationship becomes the more I understand just how easy it can be to miss something God is doing in my life. In this relationship with God, you become aware of things you may have never noticed before if the relationship weren't there. You begin to see the patterns of God's work in your life, and with each experience you start to understand God's will and how He operates. Then you will begin to look for it; you look for things that some Christians would easily miss because they have not recognized God's ways in their life.

My wife recently purchased a car because she needed something with a back seat so that she could pick up our grandchildren. The car she currently had, though it got great gas mileage, was only a two-seater. We wanted to have a stronger influence in our grandchildren's faith and being able to pick them up was important to her because she never felt comfortable driving my big truck. We prayed about the car, and I said to the Lord, "If this is something we should be doing, as you already know the main reason, we are doing this, then give us a sign and the discernment to see it."

The car was over a hundred miles away, so I wanted to get a complete breakdown of the price before we decided to make the trip. When I asked the salesman to send me the details of the price, plus all the fees, the price he sent was a little lower than the advertised price that was online. It had been lowered to $14,777 and with all the fees the price was $16,777. There was my sign, the most powerful number in the Bible—777; the number that represents the Holy Trinity of God as well as being derived from a reinforcement of perfection[1] and God's unmistakable hand in the affairs of man.

This is the kind of stuff I am talking about; the things some Christians would miss if you weren't looking for them. Again, it's just like I've heard Kevin Zadai say, "You just can't make this stuff up."

I have discovered the more I detach myself from the world, and the things in it, the more God wants to give them to me. I don't believe it is the material items that are the problem, it is the value you give to these possessions and what they mean to you. Keeping God first in everything you do and trusting Him in everything you do is the way to have everything, but the closer you get to that place the less you really want the things you thought you wanted, and the things you do want are for different reasons than you used to have. I hope I'm making sense to you, but this is how I see it at this point in my life.

Discovering who I am in Christ is an adventure and the more the Holy Spirit reveals, the more exciting it becomes. I am not the perfect being God originally made me to be, no more than Adam and Eve were after their fall from grace, but every day that passes I am one step closer to discovering who that person really is. I am watching God change me as I walk out my life and it's truly an amazing thing to see. I know that God is perfect in all His ways and everything He makes is perfect,

---

1. https://www.biblestudy.org/beginner/how-is-god-perfect.html

including me. I sometimes think to myself about how exciting it is going to be to go from being the person I am now to being who I really am someday. A spiritual being made perfect in the likeness of God, knowing that at the end of your journey you will walk into who you really are – the true you – made perfect in Jesus Christ our Lord.

There are two things I hear the most in prayer these days. The first, is Jesus saying, "Stay in me, and see where I take you." The second is, "It's not about you, but about what I can do through you."

I want no regrets when I come full circle before Jesus, back to the very spot where He thought of me and I became a living spirit. When He looks at me with those intensely powerful eyes, full of love and says, "Well done, my good and faithful servant," I want to be able to look back on my life and see that I came to the end of myself. I was faithful and the Lord was able to work through me.

Kevin Zadai once said that Jesus told him, "Kevin, what are you going to do when you're chasing me, and I let you catch me." Then He said, "Kevin, what are you going to do when I turn around and start to chase you." Thank you, Jesus, for loving us so much, and for sending us someone like Kevin Zadai to be the bridge we can all walk across, saving years of time and learning to walk in authority and relationship with you.

I can't wait to go home, but while I'm here, let's put Jesus' enemies at His feet as a footstool and bring our brothers and sisters back home. Glory be to God.

Amen.